Christmas 1997

I found this in one
thrift shops that line the way streets
of England. I nearly always find
a treasure. Love,
Dorothy

THE PERMISSIVE GARDEN

Dedicated to those who are thinking of
changing their houses because they
can no longer manage their gardens.

Corylopsis Pauciflora and
Camellia 'First Flush'

Portrait of Erica Lady Pearce, painted by her father
Bertram Priestman R.A., and exhibited at the
Royal Academy in 1925.

The Permissive Garden

Written and Illustrated by
ERICA LADY PEARCE

Foreword by
ROSEMARY VEREY

Photographs by
PAUL SCOTT

Edited by
ROSALIND AND NICHOLAS BOWLBY

SWEETHAWS PRESS

Published and distributed
by Sweethaws Press,
Owl House, Poundgate,
Near Uckfield, Sussex TN22 4DE.

© Edward Holroyd Pearce 1987

ISBN 0 9511795 0 0

Printed in Great Britain by
A. Wheaton & Company Ltd
Hennock Road, Marsh Barton,
Exeter EX2 8RP.

Editors' Note.
The editors would like to thank Mrs. Rosemary Verey for her foreword, and for all her help and
encouragement, Mr. William Bell and Mr. Tony Lord for their help with the text, and Mr. Paul Scott
for taking the photographs.

CONTENTS

LIST OF ILLUSTRATIONS

FOREWORD

Once the love of gardening has seized you by both hands it is impossible to turn your back on its pleasures, but when you can no longer plant, prune and weed as you once could, what can you do about it? Erica Lady Pearce's philosophy and ideas, which permeate the pages of this book, will set you thinking. Books have been published on labour-saving gardens and ground cover plants (a word Lady Pearce abominated), but no one until now has approached the subject of growing old gracefully in your garden and still enjoying the beauties of it in a permissive manner. The dedication says it all: it is 'to those who are thinking of changing their houses because they can no longer manage their gardens'.

You no longer worry about the work which HAS to be done, you only do the things you want to. How to accomplish this Lady Pearce has written about most delightfully from her own experience. This is a very personal book and by the last page you feel you know the author well – how she mulched to discourage weeds (her chief ally was bracken), no longer planted climbers and shrubs which demand pruning, and gave up tubs, which need regular watering. Mown grass, Lady Pearce declares, is a threat, and where possible should be replaced with paving. The early chapters tell you this and much more.

These are problems facing many people who have years of experience in a well established garden and the knowledge of how it should be done, combined with the inevitable difficulties and frustrations which beset them as they grow older. Lady Pearce's garden was on acid soil and her knowledge of her large collection of camellias, rhododendrons, azaleas, magnolias and all the acid-loving plants fascinatingly unfolds; also how she and her husband contended with the orchard and the paddock. Her comments are illuminating and sensitive.

The easy style in which this book is written is endearing and teaches many lessons: there must be flowers for picking, rhubarb is a wonderful ground cover, every cook must have a few fresh vegetables, let the primroses seed themselves, secateurs are needed every year as a Christmas present.

I feel deeply grateful to Erica Lady Pearce for finding time before she died to write so many thoughts for us, to Lord Pearce for his care in making sure the book is published, and to Nicholas and Rosalind Bowlby for editing it so carefully.

ROSEMARY VEREY

CHAPTER I

HOW IT STARTED

As one too old to do anything but deplore the general rule of permissiveness current today, it seems a contradiction to advocate permissiveness in gardens. But what else are people like me to do; without strength, without time, without a gardener? And is the result in gardens really so deplorable? I think not; and possibly this may apply to the rest of permissiveness, but that is not my subject.

The main thing is to cut out work. Land can be beautiful if nothing is done at all, provided it is looked at through the right eyes. Nature herself is wild, but few of us wish to struggle to our front or back doors through a waving field of docks and nettles. And probably the neighbours would not be pleased either.

Some control there must be, but not that of bygone times when garden help was easy to come by. Soil, climate, position make a tremendous difference and my experience is limited to a garden on a hillside, adjoining Ashdown Forest. The soil is acid, the climate cold and windy, the position high enough to have a wide view over the Weald of Kent and the South Downs. I have therefore little knowledge of things that grow in alkaline soil and sheltered places. But whatever your soil or climate, I think it is well worth trying to grow anything you want to grow at least once. I usually try twice, the second time with two of the sort. You never know what may succeed and this is the exciting and endearing joy of gardening. It makes too much work to go on trying to force plants to grow in your garden against their will. If you have no help you cannot dig out beds and change the soil to accommodate say camellias or azaleas. Try them in your ordinary soil and where you want them to grow. If they won't, give it up.

Many of us are in the position of having to cut down the work in an old, or at any rate an established garden. If I was planning a new garden, say round a new house, money being no object but in fact an investment for the future as my ideal garden would need no hired help, I would have it walled in, brick or local stone, and as much as possible of the whole area paved or bricked in and terraced if the lie of the land permitted. Gaps for growing things should be left here and there according to the wish and energy of the owner. Although patio gardens lend themselves to tubs and urns etc., this sort of gardening ends by making work because they have to be watered and should therefore be resisted on principle. That is, of course, if you try to *grow* things in the urns and tubs. If you have any urns or stone ornaments around I think they do enhance a garden.

I would never advocate flower beds against the house; I think bricks or paving stones should be taken right up to the walls. In our own experience earth against the house causes damp and dry rot inside. Climbers are also bad for the building and involve a great deal of pruning. They cover the windows, get detached in high winds and can be a great nuisance. The only excuse for them would be if a particular thing had to be hidden, but they are much better done without. You may idealise a cottage covered with roses and honey-suckle, but you are really hoping that others will admire these beauties, for you yourself will seldom see them, being mostly inside the house.

This, I believe, is one of the great fallacies of gardening. You have a garden for your own pleasure, not for others. Very few people really enjoy going round your garden. They will be polite and make appropriate remarks, but I have come to the conclusion, after over fifty years, that the majority are profoundly thankful if you omit to

E.D.P.

Garden flowers

Parrotia, Caryopteris,
Hydrangeas and Viburnum
Opulus Sterile

Symphoricarpos and Hydrangea

Spring flowers

say (on one of the rare fine days when you have visitors) "Would you like to see the garden?" But as you are obviously one of the few, being nice enough to read my book, I shall take much pleasure in telling you all about mine. It stands five hundred feet up adjoining a gorse and bracken covered common. It is surrounded by hedges of holly, oak, beech, cypress, laurel, hazel, yew, birch, brambles, bindweed, bryony - in fact an old country hedge. The extent of the land is about one and a third acres. The house stands near the common with room for a path and a narrow bed between.

When we came here, the garden was mostly grass with a few shrubs and flower beds. There was an old unproductive orchard and a small paddock, both screened from the house by holly hedges and trees. Holly hedges only need pruning once a year, make a good background with their very dark shiny leaves, and are good wind-breaks. But I don't think I would ever plant one. The fallen leaves (and being evergreen they are always falling) make weeding a painful, prickly job. Before the war, when the children were quite young, we had a gardener for one or two days a week. We had a lawn large enough for children's cricket, (balls landing in the field below counted as six and out), flower beds, and a small walled garden, once a cattle yard, where we grew vegetables. In our acid soil most shrubs and especially evergreens such as rhododendrons, kalmias and choisyas grew very well. We had a good sprinkling of these, a rock garden and an herbaceous bed.

Then came the war. Our London flat, in which we lived during the week, was destroyed in the first raid. The children and I moved to the country. The paddock, formerly given over to a shetland pony, became a vegetable garden. The pony was replaced by a goat who was meant to graze the common and provide milk, but who had a successful will to graze the vegetable garden. Hens lived in the orchard.

After the war, with gardening help getting more difficult, this vegetable garden became too large to manage. The goat had been swapped for some bees and the hens had gone. We fell for the prevailing fashion of growing Christmas trees, which were intended to pay for themselves. The paddock was then supposed to be off our hands. But the foresters' idea of weeds was not the same as ours. The twitch (or couch) grass overgrew the little trees and as this paddock is between us and the small walled vegetable garden, we could not ignore this eyesore whenever we went down the garden. Nor did it appear likely that when the trees were sold we would recover the cost of planting, let alone make any profit, for everyone else had grown Christmas trees for the same purpose as ourselves, and the market was overloaded. We did a lot of work with weedkillers and hoes and some were sold after four years but not at a profit. So we decided to keep the remainder as windbreaks for the shrubs we intended to plant in the paddock. The firs had grown very fast when we rescued them from the weeds and many were ten foot high by the time they were six years old.

The orchard, which had been used as a hen run during the war, had become covered in rank grass as a result. Something had to be done. We turned the orchard into a shrubbery with grass intakes and a central path. The lawn, never worthy of the name, we covered over with London paving stones which at that time were being sold very cheaply by Westminster City Council. Before we took this drastic step my husband and younger son tried to establish a camomile lawn. The idea was that it would never need to be cut. And it didn't, for it never grew. Either we have the wrong soil or the slugs liked the young plants too much. We agreed that as we were surrounded by green fields, we could afford to have a fair amount of stone work. In the middle of the paving we set a large pond for water lilies and goldfish, with a fountain in the middle; there is a round bed for flowers beyond it, and two smaller beds to break up the mass of stone. Most of the area we contained by low stone walls, now overgrown with heathers and rock plants. At the end, beyond the round bed, there is a bed for dwarf evergreen azaleas and a row of camellias in front of the high holly hedge that divides this garden from the orchard. I can claim that this so called "Italian" garden has been a success, cutting down the work and looking attractive the whole year through.

At the same time we turned the original black macadam paths around the house, and the grass paths elsewhere, into brick or stone paths – always laid in cement to prevent endless weeding. On the north side of the house we had mostly brick or stone patios, terraced as the hillside dropped to the field below, with three small ponds and plenty of beds for shrubs, roses and rock plants. As we were getting older and garden help was ever more elusive, it made less work to grow shrubs where before daffodils and narcissi had grown among coarse grass. So often our friends with the same problem, namely too much garden, too little help, told us that they were grassing over their flower beds and turning their garden into lawn. The man of the family considered it his job to cut the grass adding either that he found it good exercise and enjoyed it, or that he hated it, but that it had to be done. That to me is the fatal position in which to put yourself – "it had to be done".

I cannot forget the sad situation of a very old couple we knew who, on retirement, had created a dream garden round their house on Ashdown Forest. They showed us around when they were in their late eighties, but they could not get down the overgrown paths between their rare and beloved shrubs. The boy who had promised to help had not materialised, their old gardener had died, and they were unable to cut the grass themselves. I see grass in a garden as a threat - something has to be done about it from time to time. In the permissive garden you must rid yourself of any work that has to be done. Fun to do, yes; better be done, perhaps; but *has* to be done, certainly not, or the garden will become a tyrant. "We didn't want to move, but the garden became too much for us." Time and again we have heard this and it sounds very sad. After all, we ought to be able to manage our gardens so that we enjoy them. If we can't and they become a burden, it is better to leave and live in a flat.

Chapter 2

THE PERMISSIVE GARDEN

Most people have their own ideas on cutting down the work. Here are some of ours.

When planning a new garden cover as much of the ground as possible with a trouble-free surface – not grass, not ground covering plants, but stone, bricks and concrete. If practical, have walls, not hedges. Where you intend to plant, cover the earth with some sort of mulch that will keep down weeds, such as bracken, leaves, peat or straw. Make sure your compost heap and bonfire are within easy reach. If you live on a hill, place them down and not up. If possible avoid steps. These may look attractive, but they make barrow pushing difficult.

When planning a garden, have some of the beds higher than the paths. Tending them will be easier and less back-breaking. Plants that will need support should be placed near a hedge or a tree, or anything else that will save you from having to drive in a stake.

You will save yourself a lot of trouble if you do without climbers. Tying them up and pruning from the top of a ladder not only takes time and trouble but is positively dangerous. For instance I find *Pyracantha atalantioides* too labour-making by far. I do value the bright red berries that cheer the winter scene for months (the orange berried *P. rogersiana* is too attractive to my birds to last for more than a few weeks), but grown up a wall this plant has not only to be supported, but sends out so many new branches throughout the year that they

15

obscure the berries. The same goes for wisteria. I had one growing along the top of a wall – very attractive while it flowered – but it sent out so many trailers that I had to get rid of it.

As a gardener you cannot stop yourself pulling out weeds. Unless you are very active or have a small garden you will not want to take them to the rubbish dump every time. With plenty of brick paths and paved platforms you can leave them to die on the stone. I find it useful to have receptacles for weeds all over the garden. The wire cages on legs used as incinerators are ideal as the earth falls through and the weeds dry out. However, these are expensive to buy and you can make your own with plastic netting.

The real key to permissive, woodland, wild, trouble-free or whatever you like to call it gardening, is mulch. We are lucky to live next to a common from which we can cut bracken. The aim is to cover the ground with something that will discourage the weeds, not annoy your shrubs and not look too hideous. Bracken is the best answer I know. Weeds do not grow under it, shrubs like it and in my eyes it looks pleasant. It is also possible to walk on it in almost any weather. In order to cut the bracken, I wait until it is dry and brown and light. It is an ideal winter job. I take out a twelve foot length of white nylon cord with a loop at one end. White shows up well amongst the brown. Pulling up the bracken, stalk and all I wear a pair of strong leather gloves, for bracken can inflict nasty cuts on bare hands. I throw it in armfuls across the stretched out cord and when I have enough, put the other end of the cord through the loop and pull the bundle of bracken to its destination. The cord automatically tightens around the waist of the bundle. Fortunately the common is slightly higher than our garden so I pull the bracken downhill.

Having covered the ground with a good thick layer of bracken – it must be at least six inches as it will soon press down – you can throw all sorts of things on top, twigs and cuttings, clearings and leaves. Instead of putting dead house flowers on the compost heap you can hide them underneath the bracken or leave them on top if they do not offend you. It all helps and very soon you get used to the rather untidy aspect and are only too thankful to have a weed-free mattress to walk on. If you cannot get bracken you may be able to use leaves or straw or you may have to buy large quantities of peat. This will be expensive, but in the end it will save you time and money. Once you have a generous covering, keep it topped up with the clearings from your garden.

This is another reason why the wild or permissive garden is such a labour saver; you no longer have to cart all your clearings to a distant heap. You let them lie where they fall. My herbaceous border, now mixed in with shrubs, produces a lot of roughage for ground cover. Stems and leaves of peonies, phlox, lupins, Michaelmas daisies, Japanese anemones, iris etc., are cut or broken down and left, making quite a mulch by the following spring. You can grow plants that help to top up your mulch. We have masses of forget-me-nots. I don't remember how they came, but I think years ago we must have planted some. Now they have seeded everywhere. They look very pretty in the spring among the narcissi and shrubs (blue is one of the rarer colours in the garden). When they are over they can be pulled up or left where they are. In either case they add to the mulch and will grow again in the spring. Lychnis is another good mulcher. It sows itself all over the garden, even among the paving stones. It looks most decorative throughout the summer and autumn with its mass of furry, white-green stems and small but brilliant cerise flowers. It is seldom any trouble to pull up, the roots coming with the two foot stems.

Cuttings from evergreens take a long time to brown and blend, but having long-lasting leaves, suppress the weeds better than mere twigs. Branches of cypress, with their masses of feathery leaves, are splendid. I put unwanted paper and cardboard under them for they give generous cover and their weight prevents the paper from blowing about. The only prunings I do not use for mulching are the prickly ones like roses and holly. They are too uncomfortable to walk on and have to be burnt.

Nowadays much is said and written about ground cover; amiable plants that grow over your garden and keep the weeds out. In my experience almost anything that is strong enough to overcome weeds is also strong enough to overcome shrubs. Recently, I was horrified to see in a most respectable gardening catalogue *Hypericum calycinum* and *Vinca major* and *minor* recommended as ground cover (St. John's wort and periwinkle). About twenty years ago I bought them for this very purpose. They grew and they covered the ground. But they did not stop there. They fought for pride of place with less aggressive plants and shrubs and if I had not taken sides they would have won. It took two years of intermittent work to get rid of the St. John's wort, yet it would be foolhardy to claim that it had disappeared for good. Among the shrubs in the orchard, periwinkle, both *major* and *minor,* rears its head; one can't quite say ugly, because the blue flowers are very pretty, its roots intermingled with those of many a shrub. We spent hours trying to get rid of this self-inflicted pest and I don't think we shall ever succeed – especially where it has got in amongst the heather.

The only things we encourage to grow among our shrubs are London pride and dianthus. Both are fairly harmless, making mats without deep roots and are easy to get rid of when not wanted. In the permissive garden you are relying on the pseudo woodland to keep down your weeds, and shrubs much prefer to grow in this kind of environment to any ground cover with competing roots. We have now reached the stage of liking the look of ground covered with leaves, twigs and bracken. Old logs and rotting vegetation (provided it is not too green) no longer disgust me. I think they may be a shock to some orthodox gardeners, but does that matter? Certainly not in the country garden which is not overlooked.

In small town gardens it may be different. There it may be essential to rely on peat. But it is still best to pave or brick in as much as possible. There are many modern cement paving blocks which look

E.D.P.

Lilies and Hydrangea

Rhododendron 'Letty Edwards'

attractive. In fact York stone, of which the old London pavements were made and which many people pay a great deal of money for has the drawback of becoming very slippery. Outside our front door, leading to our gate, they became so dangerous that we covered them for about ten years with green roofing felt. This has the texture of sand paper and is proof against slipping. In fact it did not look at all bad and could be used with success on many garden paths.

Permissive gardening is something that most people can cope with and enjoy. Of course we would all love velvet lawns and bedding plants and brilliant herbaceous borders, but unless you have help, these things are just not on. In a wild sort of garden plants grow well because they like it that way. You can have flowers all the year round, and always have something decorative and colourful to put in vases. The permissive gardener plants wherever it suits the plant. If you have a mulch on the ground most things can be planted at anytime, because the mulch makes it possible to get on the garden whatever the weather, rain, frost or snow. When we had a gardener it was disappointing how often we were told the weather made it impossible to "get on in the garden". In a permissive garden you can "get on" when you want to.

CHAPTER 3

A TOUR ROUND THE GARDEN

And now I think it is time to take you round the garden. We are very lucky in being able to grow things all round our house, so that we can see them from the windows. This, I think, is most important, for you cannot always be in the garden and it is worth much more to you if you can enjoy it from the house. At the back door which faces north west, the path is only about three yards from the boundary hedge and the common. Here, sheltered between the house and the hedge, is the best position I can give to camellias. By best, I mean orthodox, for I find they do just as well anywhere else, but they are not supposed to get the morning sun as this causes the flowers to brown if the petals are wet or frosted.

Nearest the house is the first camellia we planted. We bought two little eighteen inch sticks from a nursery garden near Tonbridge that was selling up. I don't know the name of this camellia, but I think it is called *C*. 'Yobeki-Dori' by some nurserymen. I find that different growers call the same camellia by different names, which makes it all most confusing. Anyway, this camellia is white, fairly small, with a central boss of yellow stamens and lovely dark green leaves. It grew to a height of twelve feet in ten years. Unfortunately, during the severe winter of 1962, the heavy snow from the roof fell onto it and broke the main stem in half. Now it has grown almost as tall again. Next to this camellia is another, a *saluensisx williamsii* called 'Bow Bells' in the nursery garden where I bought it. If I had to be content with only one

camellia I think this would be it. It starts flowering in February and
continues until May. I have a *Clematis macropetala* climbing over it and
the violet-blue aquilegia-like flowers of the clematis look so lovely
with the deep rose-pink ones of 'Bow Bells' that I cannot bring myself
to cut down the clematis, though I know I should for the sake of the
camellia. 'Bow Bells' is the only camellia I have managed to propagate
from seed.

After this comes *Camellia japonica* 'Magnoliiflora': smallish, shell
pink flowers against very shiny green leaves. Next to this an 'Adolphe
Audusson', the most magnificent camellia I have with its large
turkey-red flowers. Then there is a *Camellia x williamsii*, 'J.C.
Williams,' flowering before these two last, usually in February about
the same time as 'Bow Bells,' but not for so long. Its large, wide-open
single flowers are the most fascinating dog-rose pink and no flower
could be lovelier.

Then comes a gay and useful bed growing up against the hedge in
the poor earth of the common: a *Rhododendron ponticum;* many
evergreen azaleas, which make a carpet of colour in May; a white and
green leaved euonymus; an hydrangea; pansies; Christmas roses
(*Helleborus niger*); gentian; heather; dianthus and the spring bulbs:
crocus, snowdrops, scilla, *Anemone blanda*, primroses, *Primula*
'Wanda' and fuchsia. As we use this path a great deal, it is important to
enjoy it as we go by. As it is the nearest bed to the kitchen, we also
grow the cookery essentials: mint, parsley, chives, a bay tree, and
other herbs.

Before continuing round the house, I will just take you up the path
to the garage. On one side is a small sloping lawn where we have the
washing line. (Yes, *I know*. But this "lawn" is of common grass and
wild heather, and grows so slowly that it is only cut about four times a
year. This takes ten minutes with an old fashioned hand mower).
Behind the washing line is a row of white rhododendrons and two red
ones, reinforcing the mixed hedge that runs between us and the

common and hiding our oil tanks from view. On the south side of the path there are several evergreen azaleas; a large bay laurel; choisyas; a *Pieris formosa forrestii*; a wild pink and white fuchsia; a *Styrax japonica*; diervilla and deutzia.

Back again on the path that goes round the house, we reach the north side. Below the bay laurel is a bank of hydrangeas: hortensia and lacecap, pink and blue, and a little garden on its own, leading to a cedar wood studio. Below the bank of hydrangeas is a fairly large patio of local stone with a low containing wall on the east side. A brick path leads from this to the studio. On the left of the path is a rose bed divided into two by brick steps leading to an upper patio also of brick. Steps lead up from this to join the path to the garage. In front of the studio is another patio of York stone. This was originally a sandpit for the children, then a small pond, but now paved over to make the approach to the studio less fussy. We have two other small ponds in this part of the garden. One grows bulrushes and reeds and some iris in June. The other has a few water lilies but is nearly full of blue and white iris which look lovely when they are out in June and July. Kingcups and water mint grow around the edge, and York stone surrounds both ponds. There are shrubs and trees growing all about here. Sheltered by the studio is a large *Magnolia x soulangiana,* a *Viburnum farreri* which starts flowering in the autumn and continues sparsely throughout the winter, and a *Corokia cotoneaster.* You either like this or you don't. It has tortuous, wiry branches, minute leaves of a greyish-white colour and small yellow star-shaped flowers in the summer. Mine has grown to four feet in about ten years, and intrigues most people as few seem to have seen it before.

There are wild rockeries on either side of the path that leads to the studio. The garden slopes down to the field below and the steps make it possible to have the raised beds that I like. So rock plants such as dianthus, saxifrage and alyssum cascade down the sides; there are primulas, lupins, senecio, rosemary, ferns and the ubiquitous (in our garden) small evergreen azaleas. For shrubs: *Fothergilla monticola, Prunus subhirtella* 'Autumnalis', fuchsia, skimmia and, behind, a bank of rhododendrons and deciduous azaleas.

Now to continue round the house we turn away from the north and walk along a brick path beside the east side of the house with a bank of shrubs below. Pernettya, chaenomeles, *Hamamelis mollis, Berberis darwinii, Elaeagnus pungens* 'Maculata'. I particularly like these last two together. I can see them from the kitchen window while I am doing the washing up. The masses of orange flowers on the berberis next to the gold and green leaves of the elaeagnus give that copper and brass colour which is a favourite of mine, indoors or out. Both these shrubs are easy to grow and to propagate.

Next we have a rose, 'Zéphirine drouhin', thornless, bright pink and scented. It tries to be a climber so has to be cut down often. The flower colour is very ordinary but it is marvellous not to have thorns and I have taken a lot of cuttings to grow in the paddock, and its prunings are happily added to the mulch.

Next to the Zéphirine is one of our greatest pride and joys – a *Cornus nuttallii*. In about twelve years this has grown into a tree of about fifteen feet. The flowers, green buttons in the centre of large lemony-white bracts, are lovely and unusual. The fruits are brilliant orange and the leaves, like most of the cornus family, turn a good colour in the autumn. Next to the *C. nuttallii* is an *Osmanthus delavyi* which has grown so big it has to be cut back to give the other shrubs a chance. Its leaves are small and of a very dark green, making a good background for the masses of small white flowers in the spring. The scent of these is delicious and branches of it look well in vases with narcissi. The last big shrub in this bed is a *Parrotia persica*. This is a member of the hamamelis family and if the birds would allow, the flowers are very like those of fothergilla, only pinker. But in my garden it never flowers. I have seen the bullfinch systematically pecking every bud along the waving branches. So we only grow it for autumn leaf colour, which is very fine. The bed ends in evergreen azaleas, heather, daboecia and daffodils.

All these shrubs have to stand up to the east wind as it sweeps up the field below, and the low holly hedge gives them little protection. Against the house, but still facing east, is a *Daphne odora;* four autumn-flowering *Camellia sasanqua,* their roots somewhat sheltered by a *Rhododendron* 'Britannia'; an evergreen azalea, and a *Daphne mezereum alba;* a large camellia 'Adolphe Audusson', which does very well in spite of being in the wrong position, and against the house there is the yellow winter-flowering *Jasminum nudiflorum.* In front of this bed is the old herbaceous border now invaded by many azaleas both evergreen and deciduous; *Rhododendrons* Nobleanum and May Day, a *Berberis darwinii* and a *Cornus florida rubra.* This cornus was quite large when sent by the nurseryman. For the first year it showed no leaves at all, a thing I have never known before in a living shrub. Since then it has looked better and has flowered. Of course it would like a far more sheltered position than I have given it, yet the *Cornus nuttallii,* a few yards away, has done very well.

Over the shed door, in one of our few southern aspects, there is a *Vitis* 'Brandt' which in a warm summer produces purple grapes and gorgeously coloured autumn leaves. Crowded under it to take advantage of the southern position is a *Chimonanthus praecox,* (winter-sweet). It has very few flowers, but then it is covered by the the vine for most of the summer.

The flowers in the herbaceous border that survive among the shrubs are white and yellow daisies, lupins, iris, peonies pink and red, geum, phlox, Michaelmas daisies, Japanese anemones and cranesbill. They are never staked or dug. The long stalks are cut in the autumn and left to make a mulch on the bed which is bordered by *Stachys olympica (S. lanata* -lambsear) and, viewed from the kitchen window, really does seem like an edging of silver frost. It is one of the whitest-leaved plants in the garden and the foot-length stems are useful in vases.

I have forgotten to mention a rhododendron that grows in front of the 'Adolphe Audusson' camellia. This is because it is hardly worth remembering. It is called 'Christmas Cheer' which is ridiculous because it never flowers before April, and the flowers are a very pale pinky-white. Now *R*. Nobleanum, which really does sometimes flower at Christmas, or at any rate soon after, is much more entitled to the name both for its flowering time and the cheery red colour of its flowers. Indeed I cannot praise it too highly and I have six of this rhododendron in the garden. It usually flowers in January, but if you bring it indoors, choosing the branches with the fattest buds, you will have a lovely show of crimson flowers decorating your rooms from mid-winter. It goes on flowering indoors and out for weeks. It is cheap to buy and yet few people seem to have it in their gardens.

Now we have nearly passed out of view of the worker at the kitchen sink. Here there are beds on either side of the paving stone path and steps down between two tall cypresses to a lower path that runs along the hedge. Originally these beds were sloping banks of very coarse grass amongst which narcissi bloomed during the spring. But the grass grew so rank and looked so unsightly before its yearly cut that we dug it up and planted different shrubs, leaving the narcissi to battle through.

In the bed against the house there is a double row of roses, Floribundas and Hybrid Teas. There is a terracotta coloured chaenomeles against the wall and a large hibiscus at the north end of the bed. This is covered with blue flowers during August and September and looks gorgeous amongst the roses, especially 'Fragrant Cloud' which is next to it. Hibiscus is also very good in vases.

I have heard that proximity to any member of the onion family keeps black spot away from roses, so at the edge of the rose bed there are clumps of ipheion which flower the most delectable shade of ice blue in the spring, six inches from the ground surrounded by their chive-like leaves. But I don't think they have cured the roses of black spot. The rose bed ends in a rock wall about twelve inches high and dianthus, pinks, thyme and *Senecio bicolor cineraria* grow out of it.

Opposite the rose bed is another shrub bed made from one of the original coarse grass banks. The soil here was very poor, mostly clay subsoil thrown up by the builders when making an extension to the house, but it does not seem to have made any difference in the growth of the shrubs. First, by some shallow steps, is a Woolworth cypress about eight feet high. It was bought as a miniature, but very soon proved to be nothing of the kind. It has a twin on the other side of the step. I think a cypress here and there does give a garden rather the "air" of being a garden; but the ones that have to be cut do make work. Some of the tall, thin sort do not need pruning, but in our windy garden branches get blown out of place and broken by heavy snowfalls. They grow very quickly with us. The Woolworth ones grew from twelve inches to twenty foot high in twelve years. Junipers grown from six inch cuttings reached three or four feet high over the same period. Next to the cypress is a rhododendron; then there is a *Choisya ternata,* a kalmia, a *Pieris formosa forrestii,* a rose 'Nevada' and a *Mahonia japonica.* On the hedge side of this bed are ericas, daboecia and small evergreen azaleas. On the path side there is a row of tea roses and an intermittent hedge of lavender and rosemary.

The rose bed below the house turns the corner to face our south west aspect. Here is a small sloping rockery with spring bulbs, heathers, rock plants, dwarf azaleas, Japanese anemones and *Romneya coulteri* behind. There is a terrace in front of the house and against its walls a vine grown from a seed spat from an African grape. Amazingly it has produced eatable fruit in a good summer and has grown so large that twice yearly pruning is necessary.

Opposite the terrace, and separated by wide shallow stone steps that wind up to join the front door of the house to the lower path, is a small bed packed with evergreen azaleas, flowering from April until July. Forget-me-nots, narcissi and *Lilium regale* (grown from our own

Narcissi Poeticus

*Camellia 'Lady Clare', Camellia
'Donation', Camellia Sasanqua
Papaver', Camellia
'White Swan'*

Camellia 'Silver Anniversary',
Camellia 'Our First', Camellia
'J.C. Williams', Camellia
'Comte de Gomer'

Garrya Elliptica

E.D.P.

Hydrangea 'Nigra'

*Magnolia x soulangiana
and Japonica*

Romneya and Hydrangea

Pieris Formosa Forrestii and Camellia 'Sylvia'

seed) flower among them in their different seasons. Behind, too tall now to get much protection from the low wall at the back of this bed, is the other white camellia bought at the same time as the one by the back door. Although many of its white flowers get frost-browned, its shining green leaves are a pleasure to look at all the year round.

Beyond and below this bed of azaleas there stretches to the south west a large area of York paving stone, overlooked by the windows of the house. The water lily pond with its fountain is in the middle of this pavement. On the east side there is a low containing wall over which wisteria and rock plants like dianthus, aubrieta, thyme etc. grow. On the west side there is a sloping bank above a foot high wall which grows *Erica carnea,* daboecia, dianthus, dryas and a row of small junipers.

When we first laid the York stone we left two narrow little beds and two larger square beds to break up the wide area of paving. There is also one round bed at the far end from the house. In the centre of it there is an evergreen *Euonymus fortunei* 'Variegatus,' which with its green and cream leaves is decorative all the year round. Besides the euonymus there is a ring of Fashion roses and the bed is edged by the silver leaved *Senecio bicolor cineraria.* The two narrow beds used to have tulips in the spring and bedding plants in the summer. They looked very pretty but made too much work so we bricked them over. The two square beds were originally used in the same way, but we hacked bits of root from our one yucca, planted them in these beds which they now fill, flowering every year. The yucca leaves look decorative all the time, like palm trees without a stem, and all the better for being sited in a formal garden of stone surrounds. Behind the round bed is a Portland stone group, bought from a young art student, and on either side a large urn. We used to fill these with trailing geraniums during the summer. But this meant they had to be watered and again this became too much work.

The paving stone area and this bit of the garden are bounded by an eight foot high holly hedge with a central archway and iron work gate that leads into what we still call the orchard, although it was turned into a shrub garden many years ago. The dark green holly makes a wonderful background and good shelter for a row of ten camellias. In front of them is a shrub bed with a *Cornus kousa* in the centre. This gives three shows a year and is worthy of its important position. In early summer it is covered in white, pink-streaked blossom, in late summer by strawberry-like fruit and in the autumn its leaves turn lovely fiery colours. Besides the cornus there are deciduous azaleas which give two shows, flower and leaf. In front there are many evergreen azaleas and some hydrangeas. These little azaleas are delightful plants. They grow neatly and not too big, they produce an explosion of flowers in season, their leaves are decorative all the year round and make good ground cover against weeds. In addition to these virtues they are easy to transplant, their roots growing in a compact ball, and are also easy to layer.

I must take you back now up the sloping brick path (with the heather bank on the south side) towards the front door. Here we had a small patio covered with York stones, but these became so dangerously slippery that we have now covered them with honey coloured cement blocks. In the bed bordering this patio and beside the hedge on the common side we have deciduous Mollis azaleas with sweetly scented yellow flowers in May and lovely coloured leaves in autumn. Then we have a large old *Kalmia latifolia* inherited when we bought the house, and although half of it has died and been cut down, it is still one of the largest and most beautiful shrubs in the garden and we are lucky that it has such a key position near the front door. It is an evergreen with attractive leaves, bark and growth. The blossoms, in shape and size and colour, are exactly like the old fashioned pink and white icing decorations that used to be put on cakes. Children call it the Birthday Cake tree.

Next to the kalmia is a group of hydrangeas to give colour in late summer. Then *Choisya ternata*, often in white flower but always lovely because of its mixture of pale and dark green leaves. In front of the bed, against the stone edge, *Iris unguicularis (I. stylosa)* comes out from mid-winter until spring. There is a clump of wild cyclamen fighting for supremacy with dwarf blue campanulas. At the end is a large *Magnolia x soulangiana*, which flowers abundantly every spring in the teeth of the east wind. Often its lovely white blossoms are browned but it continues to bear the few odd flowers until the leaves fall.

From our sitting room windows we can also see into a small, partly fenced garden, relic of a garage that has long been pulled down, but of which we kept some of the timbers to support climbers and to shelter a row of camellias from the east. Here there is a climbing *Hydrangea petiolaris* and a *Pyracantha atalantioides*. Climbing over these are several *Clematis macropetala, C.x jackmanii,* and others. On the other side of the fence, facing west, are five camellias, four of them imbricated (densely overlapping leaves like fish scales). Personally I do not like these so much as other camellias, though they look very impressive and solid.

Also in this little garden, making use of its wooden surrounds, are two more pyrancanthas, one of them the orange-berried *P. rogersiana,* a *Garrya elliptica,* an apricot coloured climbing rose, 'William Allen Richardson,' a salmon and cream fuchsia handicapped by the horrid name of 'Coachman', French and English lavender, rue, *Clematis montana* and *tangutica* and a white flowering summer jasmine. There is also an azara tree. It has grown rapidly and has had to have many branches cut. It now has a smooth stem and what tree men call a "lollipop" top. I think it is attractive with its very small evergreen leaves (smaller than box leaves) and tiny yellow flowers in June that have a vanilla scent. I like the scent but I have been rather put off by a gardening friend who said she disliked azara because the smell reminded her of cheap cakes.

Above the long brick path that runs down to the old orchard, with the paved garden on its lower side, was the one "pleasure lawn" we retained. Now this too has gone, bricked over except for a shrub bed at the bottom. It was not worth keeping a mowing machine for one small lawn. There were very few occasions when we used it for lazing or tea parties. We are thankful to have got rid of the obligation to cut grass and think the look of the garden is much improved. As the ground slopes down to the orchard hedge, we have designed it in three squares, about four by four yards each, descending by one step at a time to the shrub bed at the end. This new bed has filled up with all our propagations: evergreen azaleas, senecio, potentillas, hydrangeas, red-hot pokers, caryopteris, elaeagnus, pieris, choisya. In front are spring bulbs, crocus and tulips, at the back, *Prunus subhirtella* 'Autumnalis', hamamelis, fothergilla and *Corylopsis spicata*. These last three are members of the same family. It is nice for the cousins to be together. In the middle of the bed, left over from the time when it ranked as a "lawn specimen", is a *Pyrus salicifolia* 'Pendula', which looks attractive when its silver leaves show up against the dark background of the holly hedge.

On the common side of this patio, growing against a holly hedge, is a row of 'Cunningham's White' rhododendrons and very large bushes of evergreen *Azalea* 'Amoenum', *Erica carnea* 'Springwood White' and 'Springwood Pink' trespassing among them. A row of yuccas press against the brick edge.

CHAPTER 4

THE ORCHARD THAT WAS

Now we leave behind what was once a fairly orthodox garden and pass through the archway of holly with an Albertine rose forming a roof. The place we are now entering was a small orchard when we came here. The dozen or so old apple trees were picturesque but bore hardly any fruit. We tried planting new young trees, but they did no better although we paid to have them planted by experts. Not a single one of these new trees now remains, though we still have three of the very old ones. They seldom bear fruit but they make useful props for climbing shrubs, such as jasmine, roses and clematis.

Later on we started planting this orchard with shrubs and eliminating the fruit trees. Now it is so overgrown with shrubs that many have had to be moved to the paddock or cut down. Originally we had a central path of grass dividing small areas of shrubs surrounded by grass. This had to be cut frequently thoughout the summer and the central path, which slopes downhill, became dangerously slippery in the winter. So we made a brick path down the centre. Now we have got rid of all the grass intakes by spraying and handweeding among the daffodils and narcissi. Where there are no shrubs the ground is covered by bracken, leaves and twigs. The holly hedge is higher from the south side, as the ground slopes away from it and so it gives shelter from the north to delicate plants. Two evergreen *Magnolia grandiflora* 'Exmouth' bestride the central path. These magnificent magnolias are usually seen growing up the walls of stately homes, but

31

this is the best place I can offer them. The first one began to flower nine years after it was planted. The huge white flowers are like water lilies and possess the most exotic scent, not overpowering and slightly lemony. The leaves are large and decorative the whole year round.

There is a large clump of pampas grass (*Cortaderia selloana*) just inside the orchard. The great creamy plumes unfurl in late September and show over the top of the holly hedge so that we can see them from the sitting room windows all through the winter. I think they are very decorative in a garden, though I am not keen on them indoors. Very severe winds may break them down, but otherwise they last a very long time. The long grass-like edges cut your skin and must be handled with gloves on. After ten years we had to hack away at our clump to stop it spreading over the path. If you divide the root and replant it you will soon have more pampas grass than you want.

Near the pampas grass is a *Berberis darwinii*; a *Camellia sinensis* (*Thea S.*), the real tea-plant with inch-wide white, yellow-centred flowers throughout the winter; two *Camellia x williamsii,* 'J. C. Williams,' which I have already described, and 'First Flush' which really does come out early, in February, a most prolific flowerer in palest pink, which needs to be disbudded or it overdoes itself. There is a *Corylopsis pauciflora* which shines with little cowslips all over its branches in early spring, an *Acer griseum* and a sweet briar rose, 'Lady Penzance.' Climbing over an old apple tree is Rose 'François Juranville': surrounded by pink tree peonies, an *Abutilon vitifolium album*; a *Ceanothus* 'Autumnal Blue', many evergreen azaleas and lots of other things more herbaceous than shrub.

The east side of the orchard is partially sheltered by a five foot holly hedge. At the top end there is a *Rhododendron* Nobleanum and a *Magnolia hypolenca (m. obovata.)* The distinctive thing about this magnolia is the size of its leaves, at least twelve inches long and three or four inches wide. The flowers are large and white with red stamens and a very strong scent. There are several rhododendrons, a 'Corry

Koster,' 'Dr. O. Blok' and 'Goldsworth Yellow' and an *Embothrium coccineum "longifolium"*. We were determined to have this tree when we heard that it was difficult to grow. The first one we bought did die. We bought two more and one survived, which is twenty feet high and flowers every year. The flowers are orange-red giving it its ordinary name "flame tree". They are shaped like honeysuckle flowers. The leaves turn golden in autumn and are held for a long time before they fall.

Below the flame tree are some of our best rhododendrons, 'Letty Edwards,' 'Moongold,' 'Beauty of Littleworth' and *R*. Loderi 'Silver Queen.' 'Moongold' is our favourite. It has lovely bright green leaves and flowers of an exquisite lemon-green colour. Then there is *R*. Fabia, with salmon, bell-shaped flowers and dark green leaves. This is an expensive rhododendron to buy, but we have found it very easy to layer.

Behind these and far too close to the hedge now that they have grown big, is a row of camellias: *C. japonica* 'Conspicua,' very large flowers, deep rose ageing to rose-salmon; a larger flowered *C. x williamsii* 'Bow Bells' from a seedling; a *C. japonica* 'Lady Clare,' beautiful semi-double pink flowers but almost of a weeping habit; *C. japonica* 'Lady de Saumarez,' red; *C. japonica* 'Comte de Gomer,' delicate pink striped with carmine.

In spite of one of the most sheltered positions in our garden, some of these camellias being heavily leaved and six feet or so in height, have been blown loose at their roots and have had to be staked. Staking is a job I hate as I seldom hit straight and these posts are too high for me.

Among these camellias are several *Rhododendron lutescens*. The young foliage is an attractive bronzy-green making a splendid background for the primrose yellow flowers that appear from February until April or May. Then there is an ever increasing clump of *Spiraea x arguta*. The tiny white flowers appear in profusion on the arching branches in May or June. This shrub always figures in flower shows and is I suppose a good background for more solid shrubs. A pink Rambler rose, 'American Pillar,' covers an old codling apple tree and a *Desfontainea spinosa* makes little growth but produces its flowers throughout the summer and autumn. I am not very fond of this shrub but rather proud of it for being unusual. Its leaves look exactly like holly and are evergreen. The orange and red tubular flowers show up well against the dark leaves, but somehow they always remind me of the Edwardian bathing dresses that fastened below the knee.

The eucryphias are down in this corner as it is more sheltered than most places. But *Eucryphia x nymanensis* has grown so quickly and so tall that it now rises five foot or more above the hedge. It gets blown out of the ground every winter and has had to be staked. It looks lovely in July and August when covered with its large white hypericum-like flowers. Incidentally, we were told not to expect it to bloom for eight years. In fact it bloomed after it had been planted only four years and has done so ever since, in spite of the disturbance to its roots. Beside it grows a *Eucryphia x intermedia* 'Rostrevor.' This eucryphia is much easier than *E. x nymanensis*. It is more spreading, delightfully easy to layer, and not quite so tall. The flowers are similar but slightly smaller. They come a little later but continue intermittently for months, so that I am often able to use a spray at Christmas.

Down in this corner is the huge leaved *Rhododendron falconeri*. It looked so impressive at the Chelsea Flower Show that I felt I must have a try. Of course we haven't the conditions it needs, sheltered woodland, and our strong winds bat unkindly at the leaves. Nevertheless it has flowered, pale yellow with a blotch. But it never looks really happy and I would not get another.

We have several *Hypericum* 'hidcote', which grow and spread so fast that it is a job to keep them down to size. There is a small acer, a *Viburnum opulus* 'Roseum' (*V. o.* 'sterile'), a tree *Erica arborea alpina* and a *Poncirus trifoliata*, aegle for short. This last, though not a favourite of ours, attracts more notice than most of our shrubs. In May it is covered in very white opaque flowers, about one and a half inches across, that show up well against its bright green, semi-evergreen leaves. But from September until the turn of the year it is covered in small oranges. Yes, real oranges, from which I have made marmalade; though I must admit it doesn't taste very nice. The main thing against this shrub is its murderous prickles. It is said to make a good rabbit-proof hedge. I should think it would be proof against anything.

Also in this bottom part of the old orchard is a *Garrya elliptica*. It has only the holly hedge to the east for protection, but it has grown huge in twelve years and is covered in catkins during the winter months. These can be as long as ten inches and branches of this shrub make very good winter decoration. Grinling Gibbons, the seventeenth century sculptor and wood carver, used *Garrya elliptica* in some of his designs.[1]

Clethra alnifolia paniculata is not very showy and rather a nuisance in spreading too quickly, but is valuable as a late flowerer in August or September and the leaves turn a good yellow in autumn. The flower racemes are creamy white and fragrant. *Enkianthus campanulatus* grows atractively; the creamy white, red-veined flowers are small, but the autumn colour of the leaves can be very good indeed. In this place there is also more of one of my most used shrubs, *Vaccinium virgatum*. This is not only the best vaccinium for autumn colour but the red leaves are usually retained until well into the New Year. I use it for indoor decoration; the leaves survive on their stems and the branches live in water for a long time, often until the new leaf buds appear.

Now we must go back to the top of the orchard to see the shrubs that grow on either side of the brick path. Below the pampas grass there is one of the old apple trees which supports a winter jasmine and a clematis. But there is also a yellow rose, which, not having been

---

[1] This plant was not discovered in this country until the nineteenth century which presents several interesting possible solutions to the conundrum.

pruned for years, blooms at the very top of the tree, so that we can see it from our bedroom window. We saw this rose growing on the walls of Haddon Hall. It is called 'Le Rêve' and has a delicious lemony perfume. After a lot of searching I managed to get one from a rose grower in the Midlands.

Next to the apple tree is a fairly large *Hamamelis mollis*. I am so thankful that I have this one now that the original one has died which grew in view of the kitchen window and was a joy to see blooming golden for several weeks each winter. Then, after flowering magnificently (as it always did) one year the leaves failed to come out and it died, except for a lot of shoots from its roots. In my ignorance, I thought this was hazel stock, and so dug up the whole thing and burnt it. Since this catastrophe, I have learned that hamamelis is not even related to the ordinary hazel. It is grafted onto *Hamamelis virginiana*. Although not nearly as decorative, the *H. virginiana* would have been better than nothing and how I wish I had left it to take over. Hamamelis is invaluable, flowering as it does in mid-winter and unspoilt by frosts. It lasts well in water and has a lovely scent indoors or out.

To continue down the orchard: next to the hamamelis is a *Rhododendron* Praecox, a purple flowered February evergreen. It is useful indoors and outside, especially when coinciding with the daffodils. Next, a *Viburnum opulus* 'Roseum' (*V. o.* 'sterile'), the snowball tree, a *Fothergilla monticola* (far and away the best shrub in the garden for autumn colour), another corylopsis with larger flowers than the *C. pauciflora* already mentioned. This one is called *spicata*, but in spite of its larger flowers, it is not quite as attractive as *C. pauciflora*. There is a tree *Erica arborea alpina*, a *Cornus mas* (a quick growing small tree covered with small yellow pom-poms in late February), a *Prunus subhirtella* 'Autumnalis,' a *Camellia cuspidata* (bronzy-green foliage and small white flowers, very useful in vases with daffodils and tulips), a *Viburnum tinus* and a *Hoheria lyallii*.

Viburnum tinus may be common and easy to grow, but I love it. It nearly always seems to be in flower and these flowers help to puff out vases for their lace-like, pinky-white flowers against the dark green of their leaves make a good complement to almost anything. In the garden it grows fast, but neatly, and makes excellent shelter for more delicate shrubs. This is what it, and some rhododendrons, have done for the *Hoherria lyallii*, which has now shot up well over their heads, but still has shelter for its lower stems and roots. It started flowering about four years after it was planted and produces delicate white blossom every July, and is so worthwhile that I have planted two others.

Below this there are several yuccas near the path, a few deciduous azaleas and a rose, 'Blanc Double de Coubert'. This Rugusa rose flowers most of the summer and in the autumn the leaves turn gold. Above it is an *Amelanchier canadensis*. This is a small tree and the flowers in spring do not amount to much: I suspect the birds. But the autumn colour is very good. Below the amelanchier is an *Escallonia rubra macrantha,* bigger flowers and bigger leaves than the *donard* type. It grows so fast that it is hard work to keep it within bounds.

Returning up the path to the top of the orchard near the pampas grass, we now walk down again looking to our right. Immediately in front of the holly hedge is a *Cornus alba* 'Elegantissima'. We think very highly of this and are pleased that it has a dark holly background. The show is entirely of leaves: first palest green edged with white on the red stems, then changing through all sorts of subtle colours until, in the autumn, it really goes to town with every coloured leaf you could imagine, but delicate, unusual colours. Nothing could be better for indoor decoration, but I have found that the leaves soon wither in water.

Below the cornus and the evergreen magnolia is the heather bed. This stretches from the path right up to the boundary hedge and down the orchard for about twelve yards. In the heather bed there are a number of shrubs and Floribunda roses, a weeping *Acer palmatum dissectum* and rhododendrons evergreen and deciduous, among which are several Blue Tits. These are splendid little bushes. The young foliage is an entrancing pale green and the flowers the bluest of purples. But the heather has romped away. It is of all sorts and some is in flower throughout the year; and we spend a lot of time trying to free the shrubs from its exuberance. Even the supposed low-growing *E. carnea* thinks nothing of climbing over a four foot azalea. I like ericas very much. They produce flowers all the year round, are decorative in the house as well as in the garden; they keep weeds out and they are pleasant to walk on. But they do need clipping and curbing to look their best and this is something we fail to do.

After the heather bed there is a fringe of trees and shrubs round another intake which has been denuded of its grass and made into part of the woodland garden. The trees are a *Prunus conradinae,* a flesh pink cherry that flowers between February and April if allowed by the birds. The only hope I have of seeing any blossom is to bring the budding branches indoors in January and then they come out white.

There are two *Stranvaesia S. davidiana* and *S. davidiana salicifolia.* These are evergreen and have grown very quickly to over fifteen feet. The white flowers in June are not very noticeable. I grow them for the sprinkling of scarlet leaves they produce all the year round and the scarlet berries which are held well into the New Year and are useful for indoor decoration. There is also a *Prunus cerasifera* 'Pissardii', the purple leaved plum, with pink buds opening to white flowers. Again I think the birds take the buds. I find the dark leaves go very well in vases with narcissi and tulips.

A *Malus floribunda* which should look lovely in flower, in fruit and in the autumn, is also spoilt by birds. I do not use sprays or nets, they are too much work. But the birds certainly are maddening. I have two symplocos trees down here. I suppose they are between a shrub and a tree in height, but they grow taller every year; they reached six feet in only six years, flowering after two with a wonderful crop of

Oriental Poppy

*Eucryphia x intermedia and
Halesia*

E.D.P.

Rowan and Guelder Rose

Camellias 'Comte de Gomer',
'Mrs Victor Bishop', and
'J.C. Williams'

azure-blue berries. Recently the birds have taken every berry as soon as it begins to turn blue.

I call this Sex Corner for you have to have two symplocos for fertilization. Also down here is the Sea Buckthorn, *Hippophae rhamnoides,* which must have both sexes to produce its attractive orange berries, which are said not to be touched by birds. I have had four of these plants but not a single berry so I must have got the wrong sexes. Zenobia grows down here. The flowers are like big lilies of the valley and the leaves are a pale silvery green. It flowers in late July and is a valuable decorator. It grows slowly, but after ten years made a bush five feet tall and three feet wide. It is fairly easy to propagate from root shoots.

The shrubs growing round this intake are the ubiquitous evergreen azaleas, shrub roses and rhododendrons. There is a *Leucothoë fontanesiana,* an evergreen that sounds like a disease. I was given this. It is not a shrub I should ever have bought. The flowers come in small racemes like lily of the valley and the leaves are dark green. They are supposed to colour in the autumn, but mine don't.

Ceratosigma willmottianum is very worthwhile. The flowers are not profuse but in colour one of the best blues in the garden and they flower late in the summer. Then there is an aralia. This is one the most expensive plants we have ever bought. It was supposed to have huge variegated leaves, yellow and green, and panicles of white flowers. In fact the central stem died back the first winter and the original stock took over with a veritable population explosion. The country name of aralia is "devil's walking stick". This is appropriate as the stems are covered by horrible thorns. This aralia is about fifteen feet high and in view from our bedroom window. The leaves are enormous and make a bunch at the top so that it looks very tropical. The flowers are cream coloured and are so high up that they cannot be seen in detail.

I have down here a *Viburnum opulus* 'Notcutt's Variety'. I think it a pity that it cannot be called by its familiar name of guelder rose. In fact

I think the wild guelder rose just as beautiful. This grows to tree height and the glassy-red berries are attractive in the autumn. The birds propagate them everywhere.

Among these shrubs we grow many grey-leaved plants and also ericas, peonies, phlox, perennial candytuft, purple sage and everywhere we have daffodils, narcissi, tulips and hyacinths in the spring. When these bulbs grew among the grass their yellowing, ageing leaves looked unattractive for weeks as you are not supposed to cut them until they have died down. In the woodland garden the fading leaves now blend with the bracken and twigs and add to the desirable mulch.

There is another intake (these being in the nature of platforms from which you get an all round view of the shrubs) bordered by hydrangeas, mostly lacecaps, mostly blue because of our acid soil, but some blue, pink and white mixed like a country chintz. And there is a *Hydrangea paniculata,* which is like a small tree. The flower heads are rather like lilac in form, in colour white turning pinkish as they age. If it is pruned the heads become so large and heavy that the whole branch is bent down by the weight, so I think it is better not to prune and have smaller flowers that the branches can support.

Next to the hydrangeas is a *Cotinus coggygria* 'Foliis Purpurei', with purple leaves all the summer, and next to it *Cornus alba* grown only for its crimson stems in winter. It is always having to be cut down and not nearly so worth while as *Cornus alba* 'Elegantissima', which has lovely leaves as well as crimson stems.

We have a deodar tree here. It has grown very fast and now takes up too much room, but like its cousin cypress it gives a gardeny look to the place. Behind the deodar there is an *Halesia monticola* of which we are very proud. It grew into a fifteen foot tree in twelve years and is covered in snowdrop-like flowers every spring.

Below yet another clearing in which pheasant eye narcissi grow (almost my favourite flower) are several more trees: a *Ginkgo biloba,* the maidenhair tree of prehistoric interest, a *Koelreuteria paniculata,* which has yellow flowers in August, a *Nyssa sylvatica,* supposed to be the best for autumn colour. Ours does not give much of a show, but I think it is too much in the shade, being crowded by a *Pyrus salicifolia,* 'Pendula' and *Eucalyptus gunnii.*

We have six of these eucalyptus down here and they all survived the awful winter of 1962 although planted only two years before. Eucalyptus grows so fast that it is quite hard work keeping it cut down so that the foliage can be used for indoor decoration. It is excellent for this.

Stewartia pseudocamellia is a lovely tree. The flowers are very like those of eucryphia, flowering in July, but the leaves (it is deciduous) colour well in the autumn so that it gives two shows. Next to it is an *Arbutus unedo,* the strawberry tree, then a silver leaved white poplar, *Griselinia littoralis* (an evergreen with bright green leaves, but otherwise uninteresting), a *Prunus lusitanica,* a holm oak with dark green leaves, an evergreen growing into a very large tree.

At the very bottom of our old orchard, as a barrier to our neighbours, is a row of Christmas trees which grew quite alarmingly in twelve years, several cypress, bought as dwarfs but now over fifteen foot high, some rhododendrons and an enormous clump of bamboos. These make an excellent screen and shelter and a most useful source of canes for use all over the garden.

There are three more large camellias down here as well as four I have grown from seed from 'Bow Bells'. The three are *Camellia* 'Beni-Wabisuke' which has grown more than most of the camellias, but whose flowers are small, *Camellia japonica* 'Elegans' which always has masses of large semi-double pink flowers on drooping branches, and *Camellia japonica* 'Sylvia' with single scarlet flowers. This camellia is the last to flower in our garden and therefore extra valuable.

CHAPTER 5

THE PADDOCK THAT WAS

The paddock is, I suppose, about half an acre in extent. It is hedged round with holly and some beech and the hedge is reinforced by a fringe of Christmas trees to give the shrubs shelter, though as the ground slopes down to the south those at the top don't get much. At the bottom of the paddock we had a row of wild cherries, planted as four foot seedlings, but they grew so big we had to cut them down. We also, for the same reason, had to get rid of two Chilean beeches, a wild mountain ash and three cypresses.

We planted far too many trees in the paddock. It is great fun planting trees, but a temptation to be resisted unless you have extensive grounds. We got rid of a great many, but not enough, and I know now, of course, that it was crazy to plant so many. But it is a mistake we have repeated over and over again and not only with trees. All these things look so tiny when they arrive from the nursery garden it is hard to imagine they will grow quickly and become so enormous. All the same it is not a fatal mistake because you can get rid of them as need arises and you will have learnt quite a bit about them.

The paddock also has many shrubs, most of them grown from cuttings or layers we have taken ourselves. Many are duplicates of ones we have in the orchard, but not the following: *Rubus* Tridel, the thornless blackberry with lovely white flowers like wild roses; *Rubus cockburnianus* grown for its white stems in winter; *Symphoricarpos albus laevigatus,* the snowberry bush (very effective in flower arrangements); *Rosa glauca (R. rubrifolia)*, Rose 'Mermaid', *Hibiscus* 'Hamabo', *Cistus x corbariensis, Cistus* 'Silver Pink', *Abutilon vitifolium* (mauve flowers).

There are a lot of smaller things scattered about such as globe artichokes, which can be eaten and look lovely; gooseberries (planted by the birds); red-hot pokers and many herbaceous plants like daisies, echinops, ligularia.

Later we added more shrubs. *Nandina domestica* flowers in June or July. The leaves look like bamboo and colour well in the spring and autumn. It is evergreen and grows very slowly. I got an *Idesia polycarpa* because it is said to hold its berries well. Unfortunately it needs a mate to berry. I got one which died in a drought and there have been no berries. I also got a *Lespedeza thunbergii* which flowers in September and a *Cornus kousa chinensis* which is supposed to be more spectacular than the ordinary kousa, though with fewer flowers. We also got two more hoherias. They were supposed to be a repeat of the other one we had because it was such a success. One was blown down and has died. The other behaves as if it was an evergreen but does not look like the evergreen one I have seen. It flowers well and produces many seedlings.

The paddock is nearly full up. We have propagated so many of our original shrubs and many like clethra, aronia and senecio propagate themselves. The birds too are very busy spreading asparagus, goose-berries, strawberries and I am sorry to say, blackberries, everywhere.

At the bottom of our land is the small walled-in garden, once a cattle yard and adjoined by an old stone stable with three useful sheds. Beneath the north side of the wall that bounds the paddock, I grow cuttings (though I also stick these in the ground anywhere I want them to grow permanently and quite often they take root). I do not prepare the soil in any way, but the wall means that they get some protection from the wind. The most important thing for a cutting is that they should be firmed into the soil and stay that way until they have made roots. My cuttings cannot get water or any special care, but I think it would be true to say that fifty per cent of them strike. These are the things I have been successful with: hydrangeas, cistus, ceanothus, elaeagnus, *Garrya elliptica,* skimmia, hibiscus, lavender, choisya, senecio, cornus, roses.

Any rhododendrons and azaleas and many of the evergreen shrubs can be layered by placing a weight (brick, log or sod of earth) on a low-lying branch first covered with a little soil. Many others can be divided at the roots, such as yuccas, aronia, zenobia, clethra, pampas and red-hot pokers. I seldom try to grow things from seed, but we do sometimes raise things like iris and *Liliam regale* and I have grown four camellias from seed. I put the seeds in a pot or box, water them and cover with polythene as this means they very seldom (if ever) need watering before they germinate, and even after they have done so, they can still be kept moist by this method.

The walled garden is used for vegetables which will have a chapter to themselves. On the paddock side is the compost heap. Here we put all waste that will rot and not attract rats. I try to keep it topped up with a little earth and bracken, to heat it up and destroy weeds. It is usually ready for use after two years. I do not use anything artifical to quicken the process. I have two heaps side by side, one maturing, the other being used almost daily as a deposit. We empty the vacuum cleaner bags on it and ashes when we have them.

There is another smaller heap for weeds and on this I have used chemicals to make them rot. I cannot bring myself to believe that the weeds will really become harmless. I would certainly never put bindweed or twitch grass on a compost heap, or seedling weeds like groundsel, fat-hen or willow herb.

I grow two short rows of raspberries in the paddock. They seem to love growing in a bracken mulch and have never been renewed. Wires are tied across from a few stout poles which also support old, one and half inch, galvanised pipes over which we put the nets when the berries redden. The raspberry season has one very horrid repercussion. Birds become my enemies. Normally I appreciate them and think that bird song makes an enormous contribution to the attractions of a garden. I am mean about nets. Instead of using new ones every year, I make do and mend, but it is almost impossible to make them bird-proof. Rather strangely, and fortunately for me, the birds do not become much of a nuisance until towards the end of the raspberry season. I do not know why this is: whether because there is then less for them to eat or because the nets become worn and more easily entered.

I have had small birds and squirrels at the raspberries, but the chief enemies are thrushes or blackbirds. I do not really know the difference between a female blackbird and a thrush when the going is fast and furious, as it is always under the nets. But I should plump for a blackbird if I had to bet.

The stupid thing is that when I walk down the garden path throughout the year, these birds fly off squawking their warning note as if I were a danger to them. On those occasions I am not in the least dangerous. Indeed I welcome them, hoping they are disposing of caterpillars and that sort of pest. But when I get near the netted raspberries it is a different story. Very often I would not know there was a bird inside except for a sort of psychic feeling and perhaps the movement of a leaf. A bird under the net is much better at playing hide-and-seek than the grandchildren. It really hides and keeps still about it.

This is more than I am able to do. I don't know why, but I get nearer to having a stroke than at any other time I know of. My blood boils. Goodness knows what the pressure rises to. I stampede about, breaking the raspberry branches and making more holes in the net. Eventually, after several alarmingly near catches, I have to let the bird exit through my entrance. It is all very annoying and hard work and the principle reason for being glad when the raspberry season is over.

CHAPTER 6

VEGETABLES

Of course vegetables make more work than shrubs, but I cannot imagine any cook who has a garden not wanting to grow them. First there are the herbs: mint, parsley, chives and sage. Bay laurel will already be growing in the shrub garden. The only trouble-maker among these is parsley. After a time, even if you plant the mis-called perpetual, it dies off. It does need good ground and it takes five or six weeks to germinate, but parsley is so essential in cooking that it must be grown and as near the house as possible. In a hard winter I usually cover some of it under a cloche. Mint and chives grow only too well and have to be stopped from encroaching. Sage is quite decorative among shrubs, especially the purple leaved sort.

I always want to grow potatoes. I think they are a fascinating crop to plant, to dig up and to store. I plant enough to feed two people and a few visitors until the next crop. 'Duke of York' is the sort I like best. It is pale yellow when new and deliciously creamy when mashed. It is an early potato, but does the work of a maincrop as well, with a little brushing off of shoots. I keep them in an old wooden barrel, which so far the mice have not been able to enter. In hard winters I cover the barrel with old felt and bracken to beat the frost. I think it is worth keeping some potatoes for seed, though I always get some from a supplier as well.

Runner beans and broccoli are our mainstay. I have grown a bean called 'Streamline' for years and always in the same place. They have been a very reliable crop and are good for freezing. Climbing, stringless French beans are well worth a place. They are self-fertile, unlike 'Streamline' which relies on insects or spraying. They are delicious fresh or frozen, and being stringless can be cooked and frozen whole, thus saving all the work of being sliced.

I grow Swiss chard because I like the taste better than spinach. It is very easy to grow and the pigeons don't seem to like it. It does not boil to nothing in the way that spinach does and if you wish, you can use the white ribs of the leaves as a separate vegetable.

Cauliflowers, cabbages, Brussels sprouts, peas and a lot of other desirable vegetables are too much trouble for us to grow, and they don't like our acid soil. But I do grow purple and white sprouting broccoli. This, like all our vegetables except for potatoes and onion sets, I grow from seed. I transplant in wet weather which means much less work than watering in with a can. The sprouts from these broccoli last us from about Christmas time until their ground is wanted for summer vegetables. Pigeons like to strip them and so we have to use nets.

Leeks seem to me an excellent vegetable to grow from seed. Pests and birds do not attack them and they can be left in the ground all the time and dug up as wanted. Courgettes are easy too. I plant them under a glass supported by part of an old beehive, but any old bottomless box would do. I find that about four plants grown together supply our wants and are much less work when it comes to watering. For these are among the few things I do water, even when the glass lid is removed.

Many people are surprised that we can grow water cress without water. But this we have done at the bottom and dampest part of the vegetable garden for many years. The crop is not exactly luxuriant, but very convenient when I want a little.

We usually grow some lettuces and a few unusual tries for fun, such as Chinese cabbage and the much advertised Fisky V bean, both failures. I would like to grow other vegetables, but they make more work than I can cope with. I would like to be successful with asparagus as it comes at a time when there is not much else to eat from the garden. We have a small bed but it has a very poor yield; probably because the ground is acid and I do not manure it. I don't often get manure because it is too difficult to handle, and so far we have done all right without it. The funny thing is that our best clump of asparagus must have been planted by a bird at the base of one of our sheds. It comes up every year on the north side, growing between a stone wall and a stone path, without enough earth for even a weed to grow. I get more spikes each year from this root than from any on the asparagus bed. It is never watered or manured.

Globe artichokes grow all over the shrub garden, and they are too decorative just to be confined there. They produce eatable buds by hacking bits off old roots each spring and planting them in fresh places. We do not eat them much, but they are well worth growing for their silvery leaves and huge blue thistle flowers in late summer when their colour is so welcome. Eventually the dried flower heads make most distinguished indoor winter decoration.

Once you plant a gooseberry bush the birds will do all the propagating. Little new bushes are all over the paddock, some of them already fruiting. The berries have to be picked small otherwise the birds would have them all. Of course they ought to be netted, but to me are not worth the trouble.

I wish we could grow apples, but we have been so unsuccessful that we have given it up as a bad job. We still have one or two trees that sometimes bear fruit and I get a thrill when we are able to harvest our own. We grow masses of rhubarb mainly because it fills up space we haven't got time to cultivate. Its large leaves protect the ground from weeds and add a great deal of material to the compost heap. We have so much that we can be choosey in only using the youngest sticks, and these go on appearing until the end of the summer so we can eat rhubarb for over six months. It is the easiest of productive plants to grow and has thrived on the same spot since we first had a vegetable garden. In order to keep down weeds I often grow it in the paddock. A bit hacked off the yellow root usually grows with no attention. Some bits left against a wall have not even been covered with earth and still produce well. We grow tomatoes against the shed and on the south side of the cuttings wall. Given a reasonable season they fruit well, especially considering that they are never watered.

Fertilisers are out for the same reason as manure and watering and also because they are so expensive; though as gardening is a pleasure, or should be, people who enjoy messing about with fertilisers are wise to do it. Personally, I have not found it necessary having fertilised half a row of vegetables and left the other half without, and the fertiliser has made no difference at all. Our soil, like so many, needs potash. Potash is very expensive to buy but now so many of our shrubs and trees have to be cut back we can get most of what we need after making a bonfire of their branches.

Perhaps I ought to include wild strawberries in this chapter on vegetables. We got a few plants because they are a delectable fruit and provide good ground cover. I can certainly vouch for the latter. The whole ground is covered by wild strawberries now and we expend much energy trying to get rid of them. They are delicious to eat if you get them at the right time, but they are very tiresome to pick and no one does so except the grandchildren. I would certainly not advise anyone to import them into their garden. They not only spread by their own runners, but birds carry the seeds everywhere as they do with most of the berrying plants.

CHAPTER 7

FLOWERS FOR INDOORS

Besides getting a lot of enjoyment from our garden and seeing how "they" are all getting on, I expect it to provide us with flowers for the house all year round. Shrubs need hardly any arrangement, but they do need fairly large, heavy vases that will not fall over. The trouble is that vases are often the wrong shape, and many of my heavy ones are so wide at the top that I have to stuff in lots of things to hold each other up. I know I could use a ball of wire netting or a pin stand, but I never do. A very good present for anyone who likes house flowers would be a tall, narrow, heavy vase. These take some finding but are really lovely things to possess. Any container that will support one decorative branch means no fussy flower arrangement, but a simplicity that would look distinguished almost anywhere. I do have one favourite vase that is almost always in use. It is cylindrical in shape, only eight inches high, banded at the top and bottom with a dark metal strip and decorated in between with blue and white oriental figures under a blue grey-glaze. It is from China or Japan. In my possibly prejudiced eyes, it enhances almost anything in it. Perhaps it is at its oriental best with those most oriental shrubs, winter sweet, hamamelis and magnolia.

Of course there are flowers as well. In the spring there are daffodils, narcissi, tulips and bluebells; in the summer ixias and iris, daisies and phlox; in the autumn, Michaelmas daisies, kaffir lilies. Many of these look at their best mixed with the scarlet-stemmed cornus or grey

Looking south over the Weald to the Downs in the distance.

Shrubs thriving in the subsoil thrown up by the builders on the south side of the house.

The water lily pond with its fountain on the south-west side of the house.

A resident of "The Orchard That Was".

Looking towards the house from the south-west.

A pond near the studio on the north-east side of the house.

Towards the vegetable garden with the Downs in the distance.

The view from the terrace, looking south.

The Permissive Garden in the spring.

The path leading to "The Orchard That Was".

Euonymus and *Cornus kousa*.

The path leading towards the studio on the east side of the house.

senecio, and I love the purple-leaved plum, *Prunus cerasifera* 'Pissardii' to give it its full name, with narcissi and tulips.

Flower arrangement is such a personal thing that I am quite averse to being told what to do. I like vases full of different things. Bunches of all the same sort, sold by most florists, are to me very dull by comparison. When I take a nosegay of mixed shrubs to a friend in hospital, I have been greatly encouraged by the complimentary remarks of all beholders. And of course most shrubs last much longer in water than most cut flowers. As for the business of arranging them, for those who enjoy it the time and trouble is not wasted, but most shrubs need little or no arrangement.

I find it is impossible to predict which flowers will last well in water. Two branches of hydrangea, picked at the same time from the same plant will behave differently, one dropping almost at once, the other lasting for a week or more. Even standbys like eucalyptus and senecio cannot be guaranteed, though they do not often fail. I have found geums and tradescantia are long lasting in water, whereas 'Esther Read' daisies and sweet williams are not.

I am too lazy to go through all the paraphernalia of smashing some stems and dipping others in hot water. As they are all picked from the garden and I can get more, I merely put them in water and hope they will last. Of course the temperature of rooms makes a big difference, which is the reason that hospital flowers droop so quickly. Camellias in tight bud are good for long stay patients. Usually the leaves last for ages and with a bit of luck the buds will come into flower.

I am not fond of dried flowers though I have seen some beautiful and skilful arrangements, and I think things like globe artichokes and honesty are more decorative dried than in flower. I do use dried hydrangeas amongst live shrubs. Their blue-green colours are very helpful, especially with red berries and grey leaves, and during the winter months there are not many blue flowers about. I use them with other shrubs so that they are in water, but they can be used without water. I never dry them specially. They usually retain the colour they had in the garden if picked late in the year.

Senecio bicolor cineraria, a much divided grey leaf, sometimes almost white-blue, is to my mind the most useful decoration in the garden. In vases it enhances almost anything it is put with. Small leaves torn off greatly help in table arrangements. A fringe round a mixed posy has the effect of lace round a Victorian bouquet. Larger branches help to lighten and beautify other shrubs. I used to use the *Senecio greyi*, before I found that *S. bicolor cineraria* was just as easy to grow. *S. greyi* has all the good points but its leaves are not divided and don't give the lacy effect that I prefer. Both these senecios come from hot dry places. They seem perfectly hardy here so long as they are never water-logged. The *S. bicolor cineraria* seeds itself all over the garden, especially between the York paving stones, so I think it must like lime. If you leave it in water it will develop roots and can be planted outdoors.

During the winter I am particularly proud of a display of *Camellia sasanqua* seen from the kitchen window. We have four here, two pink and two red, planted against the house, and they have grown so quickly that one of them blooms two feet above the window, against the glass. They begin to flower in October and continue until March. It is not much good giving the names of camellias because the growers have their own names for them. A neighbour grows a sasanqua which she calls *C. oleifera*. It is very beautiful, white tinged with pink. I have tried to get one like it with no success.

Camellia sinensis (Thea s.) begins flowering in October and continues throughout the winter. Out of doors the white, yellow-stamened flowers get spoilt by frost and rain, but budding sprays flower very prettily indoors. As this is the true tea plant I have tried to make tea from the dried small leaves. It tasted of tea, but not very nice tea.

Elaeagnus pungens 'Maculata' lasts well in water, but the yellow in its leaves is almost too strident for most rooms. *Vaccinium virgatum* is one of my favourites in winter vases. The red leaves do drop off eventually, but the sprays never look unattractive and if they are left in water the pale green shoots develop into their little spring flowers. *Prunus subhirtella* 'Autumnalis' flowers in the garden during the winter, but if brought indoors makes a much more impressive show. I often use it with holly or skimmia at Christmas and like to think it has the effect of snowflakes among the red berries. *Hamamelis mollis* is a standby for several weeks during the winter. It grows attractively (though very slowly), smells delicious and needs no arranging so long as you do not overcrowd the vase. There is *Garrya elliptica*, one of the most distinguished decorators with its long drooping catkins of distinctive design.

Eucalyptus is useful throughout the year, provided that you remember to keep it cut down so that you can reach the foliage. The young leaves are particularly attractive and delicate, of a bluish, whitish colour, before becoming more ordinarily shaped narrow leaves. But they still maintain their attractive colour and usually last for a long time in water.

Pernettya retains its pale pink, white or red berries, throughout the winter and the birds do not seem to eat them. The very small, spiky, dark green leaves make a good foil for the pale colours of the berries. *Skimmia reevesiana* is another of my favourites. In a vase with *Senecio bicolor cineraria*, its red berries look very gay and both last a long time in water. I usually use skimmia instead of holly for Christmas decoration. The berries are brighter and they have no prickles on their green leaves. My birds do not seem to eat skimmia berries, but a neighbour complains that hers do.

Symphoricarpos albus laevigatus, with its large white berries, often held throughout the winter, can look most attractive, especially in vases with blue-green hydrangeas and eucalyptus or cineraria. Symphoricarpos, more simply called snowberry, grows wild in the hedges in many parts of the country, but I have not found it near us and so bought mine. It is easily propagated either by seed or root cuttings and grows all over our paddock.

Stranvaesia davidiana and *S. d. salicifolia*, although having hawthorn-like flowers in spring, are more useful for their red berries and occasional red leaves during the winter. *Viburnum farreri* and *V. tinus* both flower more of less continuously thoughout the winter. A branch of the former looks delightful on its own, but *V. tinus*, with its very dark leaves, needs something to lighten it.

Helleborus niger, the Christmas rose, is not of course a shrub, but I cannot resist growing it for Christmas table decoration. The short stems wedged into moss–lined saucers carry such beautiful flowers. I grow it against my north wall in the vegetable garden with a piece of glass or polythene over it to protect the flowers from frost or rain damage. The kaffir lily comes into flower in late autumn and continues for a long time. I find it the greatest help in vases. It is like miniature gladioli and as long as the spent flowers are removed, it lasts well in water. You can get in in several colours, but I only have the scarlet one which I much prefer. The flowers tend to fade to pink indoors. It amazes me that such a delicate flower should bloom so well at this time of year.

When I first had a garden I used to bring ribes, (flowering currant) into the house during the winter. Indoors the flowers came out white, prettier than the rather purple-pink they flower out of doors in the spring. But ribes gives off a strong and rather stuffy smell which I dislike, so I never use it now. There are so many flowering shrubs that can be brought on to flower indoors. Besides the regular standbys, there are a lot of other shrubs in bud that will come out in water. Chaenomeles looks charming in an oriental vase.

It seems strange to me that so many winter flowers should possess some of the strongest and most exotic scents of the year. *Hamamelis mollis*, though slightly reminiscent of lanoline ointment; *Viburnum farreri*, almost stuffily sweet; *Chimonanthus praecox*, powerfully scented; *Daphne odora*, even more so; *Mahonia japonica*, like lily of the valley. Maybe it is because there are so few fertilizing insects about that they have to make this big effort to attract them.

By February winter is really over in the shrub garden. *Rhododendron* Nobleanum will be in full flower. *Camellia x williamsii* 'First Flush' will certainly come out into pink flower if brought indoors. The trouble with this camellia is that every branch is crowded with buds so, unless you disbud, there are too many flowers for its own good and too many to look its best. All the same it is lovely and a wonderful "herald of spring". Also in February another *Camellia x williamsii* my favourite 'Bow Bells' comes out. The trumpet-shaped flowers are a lovely shade of pink, scented and very profuse, though not to the extent of having to be disbudded, and it usually flowers until May.

Cornus mas has tiny yellow flowers and in our garden it has grown into a small, but spreading tree and is always having to be cut back. Forsythia flowers are decimated by birds, but in this instance I am grateful to them because I prefer to look at a few rather than a mass of these bright yellow flowers. Apparently yellow is an attractive colour to birds. It is said that they always go for yellow crocus rather than the other colours, but I have never known them to spoil the lemon-yellow corylopsis which flowers from February onwards, nor for that matter the winter yellow flowers of *Hamamelis mollis, Mahonia japonica* or *Jasminum nudiflorum*.

We grow *Daphne mezereum,* or really I should say that the birds grow it for they find the berries so attractive that they deposit them all over the garden. They do not propagate *Daphne odora,* the peculiarly sweet scented one, though this is easily grown from cuttings and is worth growing for its scent alone.

Pussy willow, growing wild on the common outside the garden, is something I always bring in to decorate the house – silver and gold together make a lovely combination and of course willows last well in water. Narcissi are usually out at the same time and these two mix well. Corylopsis looks lovely in vases; *C. pauciflora* is the prettiest I think, but with us it is not nearly so hardy as *C. spicata*. This last increases fast by root cuttings. The flowers are larger than *C. pauciflora* and the lemon-yellow is tinged with green. Branches look very Japanese in tall vases.

Most of the camellias flower out of doors towards the end of a mild February. 'Preston Rose,' 'Adolphe Audusson', *C.* 'Magnoliiflora', *C.* '*Dobrei'*, *C.* '*Jano'*, *C.* 'Beni-Wabisuke, and *C. x williamsii* 'J.C. Williams'. This last, a single flower of the most beautiful dog-rose pink with yellow stamens is outstandingly lovely. A little later, *C.* 'Elegans', 'Lady Clare,' 'Donation,' 'White Swan' flower. The latest of all with me is 'Sylvia', the single brilliant scarlet. The *Camellia japonica* 'Mathotiana' and its variants are not my favourites, being too formal. At the same time they are impressive. *Camellia cuspidata* which has grown ten feet high in ten years and produced several seedlings, goes perfectly in vases with narcissi. The evergreen foliage is bronzy and delicate and the small white flowers are prolific. 'Cornish Snow' is another camellia with much the same characteristics. 'Donation' is written up as an exceptionally beautiful camellia. It is pink and semi-double and certainly very attractive, but I do not consider it better than many of the others. If you grow roses and camellias it is possible to have one or the other for indoor decoration throughout the year.

The mauve or rosy purple *Rhododendron* Praecox usually comes into flower at the same time as the daffodils, and together they make a delightful colour mixture. *R.* Praecox is only a semi-evergreen, and the leaves can look rather unhealthy.

March is often one of the worst months of the year, but there are usually days of pure joy thrown in among the many dreary ones. All sorts of things are stirring in the garden and there is no excuse for not having colour in the house. The February flowers are mostly still there, many of them more fully out, such as *Garrya elliptica,* whose catkins grow longer and more impressive as they age. Most of the

Camellia japonica cultivars are in flower, and unless the weather is unusually severe, by April the shrub garden is fully alive again.

When the spring outburst is over it is interesting to count the flowers that keep going throughout the summer. I think these are perhaps the most valuable of all. If you have acid soil and grow shrubs you can hardly avoid a wonderful display from April until the end of May, but by late June, the azaleas, rhododendrons, camellias and magnolias, pieris and a host of others will be on the way out. There will be a spattering of later flowering rhododendrons such as 'Purple Splendour' and 'Sappho'. However, the roses will be coming out in their first impressive burst of form and colour. At this time I realise that I am inclined to underrate the rose. One could not possible do without it although it makes more work that most shrubs, does not look good for half the year and produces unattractive thorny cuttings. Our roses never get manured, sprayed or watered and they are cut down like any other shrub. And yet they do give us the most lovely show, both outside and inside the house.

No, an English garden cannot do without roses, especially ones that flower throughout the summer like 'Queen Elizabeth', 'Zéphirine drouhin', 'Paul's Scarlet climber', the Floribundas and Hybrid Teas. 'Nevada' gives two stupendous shows and several of the so-called shrub roses like 'Blanc Double de Coubert' flower throughout the summer.

By July the eucryphias, potentilla, hoheria, romneya, ceanothus, caryopteris and cistus are probably in flower. In August *Ceratostigma plumbaginoides,* escallonia, jasmine, clematis, yuccas, cotinus, hypericum, kniphofia (red-hot poker) will be out.

There are not so many shrubs that flower in the autumn except the great standbys, the hydrangeas. The climbing hydrangea comes out first usually in June. The others begin towards the end of July and keep on flowering until the frosts get them when they turn the most sophisticated colours, bluey-purple, purple-green, rose and maroon, green and silver. You can never be sure what they will do next, but the flower heads are a great asset indoors. Hydrangeas are delightfully easy to propagate: a piece with a heel taken off a stem and firmed into the earth will usually produce a flower the following year. Our soil being acid tends to produce blue flowers, but most of the cuttings are started beneath our north wall and I suppose that because of the lime mortar from between the bricks, they nearly always flower pink until moved into their permanent places. There they go through a change of colour, eventually becoming shades of blue.

Lespedeza thunbergii, fuchsia, nandina, hibiscus, *Catalpa bignonioides*, clerodendrum, and koelreuteria all flower in the autumn, but the best colour is in the leaves. When *Forthergilla monticola* is in the full pride of its gold and scarlet heart-shaped leaves, there is nothing to touch it for sheer brilliance. However, all fothergillas do not colour equally well; we were so thrilled by the first that we bought another. It is in a different part of the garden, but its leaves turn only to yellow. On the other hand, root cuttings I have taken from our original plant turn the same brilliant colour as their parent.

Liquidambar and nyssa, both trees, run it close. The American paper birch with its white-barked trunk is an exotic sight when its leaves turn brilliant gold. Most of the cornus family produce lovely coloured leaves and so does *Parrotia persica*. Its cousin, hamamelis, sticks to old gold, and so do a lot of the others. *Amelanchier ovalis (A. vulgaris)* usually provides many lovely colours in the autumn. *Robinia* 'Frisia' is an astonishing brilliant yellow throughout the spring, summer and autumn. This seems to me an excellent tree for any garden, but is not easily obtainable for some reason.

The deciduous azaleas, or rhododendrons as they are now supposed to be called, turn as good an autumn colour as could be wished for, well able to compete even with fothergilla. They also provide a spring show of the most gorgeous coloured flowers. A few years ago, we bought several plants simply for their autumn displays. *Ampelopsis heterophylla* (now *A. brevipedunculata*) is a vine of sorts. The berries are small, but a lovely cerulean blue and the leaves colour gold. The birds don't seem to eat these berries. It really needs something to climb up which is a nuisance, and most of ours are trailing over the ground.

Besides the leaves there are many berrying plants that make good indoor decoration. *Cornus nuttallii* has the most fascinating orange seeds decoratively packed. Halesia has curious shaped yellow ones, *Rosa glauca* (*R. rubrifolia*), large bright red hips like the wild hedge roses. The brilliant red leaves of *Vaccinium virgatum* and the silver ones of cineraria, look very good in a vase.

If you like pale mauve as a colour (which I do not) hebe, or veronica as it used to be called, flowers pretty well throughout the winter. It also sows itself all over the garden and unless you pull up the seedlings when they are very small they root deeply enough to make removal difficult. This also applies to *Leycesteria formosa,* except that the flowers are a maroon and pale cream colour. The country name for leycesteria is 'Granny's Earrings' and you will see why if you grow it. A plant was given us by a friend. The maroon berries are a deeper shade than the flowers, but they must be attractive to birds who have planted it all over the garden. We get rid of it when we have the energy.

Iris unguicularis (*I. stylosa*) is a welcome addition to winter table vases. I have had a clump for years near our front gate. I pick the short stemmed buds as soon as there is any colour to be seen. They come out in water and their mauve-blue flowers with the bright yellow streak are truly exotic in an English winter, especially if they are mixed with pink camellias, which is perfectly possible as the *C. x williamsii* are usually in flower at the same time.

CHAPTER 8

CHITCHAT

Time has passed since I began to write about our garden. We have had to cut down many more shrubs and move others. Our shrubs grow very quickly. They never have any fertilisers and the only encouragement they get is the occasional mulch of bracken. Our soil is classed as "hungry" in agricultural parlance and most of our shrubs have had to endure very cold winters and summer droughts, but very few have died. Strangely, the hydrangeas have survived well, and the established camellias.

We do a lot of cutting back to keep our paths clear. When we suggest secateurs for Christmas presents, the family become incredulous and tend to remind us that they gave us those last year. Long handled cutters are extremely useful and designed to cut tougher branches. We use a very long handled tool called a "Squol"; it is very good for scratching up weeds from under shrubs.

Bluebells have invaded our garden to a now disastrous extent. I think they must have come in from the common, though there do not seem to be many there. At first we thought they looked delightful growing round the shrubs in spring. But now these bluebells have become beyond a joke. They grow as thick as grass in the spring and the flowers are beautiful. They die down after the spring burst, and we forget about them until the following spring when they come up thicker than ever. When you turn over the earth the tiny white new seedlings are everywhere, and a mature bulb, is often bigger than the average daffodil bulb. I feel these must take a lot of nourishment from the earth around our shrubs, and we have a programme for eliminating them. So far it has not got very far. We have been told that if you cut off the heads before they flower for two seasons running, you will get rid of them. We tried cutting them with the sharp edge of the useful "Squol", but we cut them too soon and they all managed to flower later on.

Lately primroses have seeded themselves everywhere, but these are one of my favourite flowers and most welcome. I don't know where they came from; there were a few on the common and I suppose they seeded themselves and liked what they found in our ground.

We have the usual host of weeds to deal with. If the mulch is thick enough most of them are discouraged, and by and large we are able to deal with our weeds, some poisoned, some dug out and many hand-weeded, which is quite fun when you are in the right mood. We have been lucky not to have ground elder, but have had most of the others. We made a dead set at docks and creeping buttercups and twitch grass, but they still recur.

Lesser willow herb with its millions of air-borne seeds is all over the garden, especially hidden under other things and managing to look exactly like a sweet william for a long time. It has the title "Weed of the Year" with us and continues to earn its name. It is very closely run up by my husband's "Little Enemy". The English name is Hairy Bitter Cress, Latin name *Cardamine hirsuta*. The tiny stem grows out of a small rosette and the seeds are contained in thin pods that burst audibly (if you are near enough) with a little click. They seem to have such a short growing cycle that they can cover the ground in no time at all.

We have, of course, masses of sheep's sorrel, a weed that invests acid soil and has very long, wiry, yellow roots. Bindweed is infuriating. When it escapes early detection and a large white flower appears at the top of a rhododendron, it is as beautiful as any in the garden and

I feel foolish for wanting to be rid of it. But when I dig up the horrid white root, thick and knobbly, I detest it. In fact, if I am in the right mood and the soil is in the right condition, mining for bindweed roots can be a rather satisfying job. Once the white root has been found, it is fairly easy to follow its path in the dark earth. But it is also easy to break the root and sometimes to "lose the scent" altogether.

Brambles and bracken are always about the place. Brambles love rooting at both ends, but with stout gloves and optimism it is possible to make a rewarding onslaught. Pulling up bracken is a finicky job, but at least the bracken can be used again as mulch.

Of the many things we have imported and which have now became a nuisance, I must add: yellow garden loosestrife, lemon-scented balm, blue bugle and feverfew, or to give its Latin name, *Tanacetum parthenium* (*Pyrethrum p*.). The loosestrife, balm and the feverfew, have roots that are very difficult to pull out. That is why I am so grateful to lychnis. The whole plant, root and all, usually comes with one gentle pull and this also applies to forget-me-nots.

Our soil must have been infested for generations with foxglove seeds, because however often we remove the large-leaved plants before they seed, there are always plenty to take their place the next year. We dare not leave them undeterred for fear that they will take over completely. Sweet williams abound in our garden. We collect their seed, (especially the salmon-pink ones) and scatter them wherever there is any space. They make pleasant colour in the summer, sow themselves, and, like lychnis, are very easy to pull up. Nasturtium, once sown, come up all over the place, but they too are easily got rid of. The first strong frost reduces them to a harmless mass of white strings. They come up solidly every summer and cover the vacant ground where the potatoes have been, but I have never thought of them as an enemy. In fact they have lovely flowers and prevent weeds from seeding.

I am growing knapweed and bergenia to keep down weeds. The

knapweed has pretty blue flowers and attractive leaves and spreads quickly; it can become a nuisance. Bergenia leaves are so large that they should keep the ground under them clear. The pink flowers, borne on spikes, are a welcome bonus.

It is possible to buy alpine strawberries guaranteed not to have runners. Mine certainly have runners, but with our experience of their ability to over-run everything, I would have no truck with them. Even if they don't have runners the birds plant the seeds everywhere.

Compost makers are warned that sycamore, plane and chestnut leaves are no good in the heap as they do not decompose, but they make excellent and lasting mulch on shrubbery paths. We have to do a lot of branch cutting in the orchard and paddock. These branches can be left where they fall in the wild garden, but they are much more welcome additions if they are cut before getting too big and difficult to lop. However, we never remember to do things in time and if the branches have grown unwieldy it is best to cut them into smallish pieces so you are not always tripping over them. If you can cut them up while they are still on the tree it is usually easier than cutting them up on the ground; it is also a job that can be done at any time of year and in any weather.

If you have a lot of paving, as we have, you are almost sure to be troubled by algae. It can make the stones look dark and unattractive and also slippery. We have found that a good, and comparatively cheap, way of keeping algae down (I don't think you can ever get rid of it completely in our climate) is to brush it over as hard as possible with a long-handled garden broom dipped in a bucket of household detergent and water. Although we have used quite a strong solution, it has had no harmful effect on the rock plants growing on the stones, such as aubrieta, dianthus, alyssum and senecio.

With us there is the added worry of the central pond which is about a foot below the level of the paving, in two descending steps. So far there have been no ill effects from the detergent. Indeed the water lilies could do with quite a lot of thining out. The water is completely hidden by their leaves in the summer. We ought to have reduced the roots every other year or so; in fact we have only done it once since the pond was made. Digging up water lily roots is quite a hard job, but apart from that (and we have been apart from that!) a pond is no trouble at all. We used to keep goldfish in it and they caused no trouble either except that when the water was iced over in a hard frost we made holes in it for their sakes. Sadly a heron took all our goldfish in two swipes and we did not think them worth replacing. Our water lilies are the red 'Escarboucle', the large white 'Gladstoniana', the yellow 'Marliacea Chromatella' and the pink 'Firecrest'. The flowers are extremely beautiful and on occasions I have used them for table decoration. They are supposed to stay open if you cut off the stalk and pour wax into the cavity. I have not been very successful with this method, but with luck the flower remains open for an hour or two. The fountain is controlled by a switch in our sitting room which overlooks the pond and the whole of the paved garden. We only put it on for fun, grandchildren or visitors, but the statue group to which it is attached is always decorative.

If your garden soil is acid and you want to grow rock plants which normally prefer limestone country, try to get some York paving stones to use up some of your space, preferably embedded in cement so that you don't have to weed in between. We have found that many plants seed themselves on these York stones, which I imagine come from limestone country. I do know many people in the limestone dales of Yorkshire who have wonderful rockeries. Aubrieta, alyssum, dianthus, senecio, cineraria, lychnis, *Erica carnea,* ampelopsis, prim-roses, and the miniature iris (wait for it - its official name is sisyrinchium!) have all seeded themselves on our paving stones.

I was given a plant of rue some time ago. It has lovely blue-grey leaves and would look beautiful in vases, but it has such a repellent smell that it is impossible to use indoors. Like other grey plants it needs a dry site.

We grow the ordinary lavender and the 'hidcote' variety which is dwarf and has a darker blue flower; and what we used to call French lavender. Its proper name is *Lavandula stoechas* and there is a green form as well as the silver leaved one. But I prefer the latter. And there is rosemary which should grow in every garden for old times sake.

If anyone wants a really fast growing tree, I would recommend the white poplar. I pulled up some suckers of this from the road side and in a very few years they grew into fifteen foot trees with a very pretty maple-shaped leaf, grey-green on top and white below. But they produce innumerable suckers and need watching.

I have found that *Mahonia japonica* roots very easily from cuttings. We have many bushes of this now as a result. I pull off the two to three foot side stems and stick them in the ground and often they "take", and grow into another bush. I even did this sucessfully in a drought. The will to live seems as strong in plants as in humans, but not all, of course. Some things are very hard to propagate. We have never had any luck with *Rhododendron* Nobleanum, and kalmias are difficult. Anyway, it is great fun trying especially if you are told it is impossible.

As your trees and shrubs grow they will all help the mulch and you will be less dependent on bringing in things such as bracken, which is certainly a labour. I enjoy getting it, but then I am lucky to have it so near the garden. To me it is an ideal winter job and I feel it is doing my dear plants so much good.

I think if you have an unorthodox garden like ours, it is a good thing to grow as many unusual plants as you can. It distracts people and as they look with curiosity at some shrub or flower they have never seen before, they forget that you haven't got a lawn or any neat formal flower beds.

A keen gardening friend who lives in East Anglia and has the right soil for rhododendrons and so for the same shrubs as we grow, made a list of those seen in our garden which he had not got and wished to grow. Although many are far from rare and I have already mentioned most of them I am appending his list:

    Aralia
    Clerodendrum trichotomum fargesii
    Clethra alnifolia 'Paniculata'
    Cornus florida
    Cornus kousa
    Cornus nuttallii
    Embothrium
    Eucryphia x intermedia
    Halesia monticola
    Hoheria
    Hydrangea paniculata
    Idesia polycarpa
    Kalmia latifolia
    Koelreuteria
    Lespedeza thunbergii
    Magnolia hypoleuca (*M. obovata*)
    Magnolia sieboldii
    Osmanthus delavayi
    Parrotia persica
    Poncirus trifoliata (aegle)
    Ptelea trifoliata
    Rubus cockburnianus
    Stewartia pseudocamellia
    Vaccinium virgatum
    Viburnum plicatum 'Mariesii'

My own list of the more unusual shrubs would include:

    Abutilon vitifolium
    Azara
    Camellia cuspidata and *C. sinensis* (*Thea s.*)
    Corokia cotoneaster

Mixed flowers

Camellia 'Adolphe Audusson'
and Magnolia

Rhododendron Nobleanum

Spring flowers

Summer flowers

Symphoricarpos and Hydrangea

Rhododendron 'Mayday'

Eucalyptus and Echinops

Desfontainea
Disanthus cercidifolius
Enkianthus
Ginkgo biloba
Hibiscus
Hydrangea heteromalla H. bretschneideri, H. paniculata,
H. 'Nigra' and *H. quercifolia*
Nandina
Nyssa sylvatica
Oxydendrum
Zenobia pulverulenta

Chapter 9

OLD GARDENING TALK

Although I set out to write about a garden that needed very little upkeep, I realise that I have been talking about shrubs and growing things: in other words, old gardening talk. I couldn't help it because I love gardening; but if you are getting old or too busy or see the day coming when you must cut down, it is sensible to prepare for that time. You must not let yourself get into the position when you have to leave your home because the garden is too much for you.

In the country, most people have too much land round their houses. Even the young and energetic are always trying to get labour saving helps: sit-on mowers, electric hedge cutters, power-driven rotorvators. We've been through all that. These things can be a help, but you don't want to be dependent on them: they often go wrong and need a lot of servicing, besides being quite an effort to use.

One of our sons has two or three sheep to keep his grass down. This has been a great success, but he lives near a kindly farmer who himself keeps sheep and in exchange for the lambs and the wool assumes responsibility for their mating, dipping and shearing, and keeps an eye on them when my son is away. For some people with too much grass, keeping two or three sheep might be worth considering.

Basically, however, you need to be independent of outside help to feel secure. We are lucky that as our garden is on a slope, the orchard, paddock and vegetable gardens beyond cannot be seen from the house. This I think is terribly important. You must not be able to see from your windows a garden that becomes a worry. If your garden is flat, I suggest paving round your house to give you a feeling of space or at least of a courtyard. Of course in paving I would leave small places in which, however incapacitated or busy, you will cherish some of your most loved plants.

The usual reaction to this idea is that it would be far too expensive. Yet often the people who say this are prepared, as an alternative, to move to another house. And believe me, this would be far, far more expensive in money, time and health. There are many different types of paving to be had today, some, usually bricks, even second hand. There is gravel to be considered and even macadam. All are suitable if properly laid down. Some people hate paving. My youngest sister, contemplating buying a house with a garden already largely paved, remarked, "The first thing I should do would be to take up all that paving". We stared in horror and implored her, "Do wait at least until you see how much gardening you are able to do". If you have a garden beyond your paving, you must do something to keep it out of sight. If you get going soon enough you can build a wall. The point is that you must do something to hide from view a piece of ground that is going to cause concern.

I have mentioned many shrubs and trees that we have in the hope that they might be useful. A mixture of evergreens and deciduous looks best; as far as possible giving colour interest and leaf variety throughout the year. You will enjoy deciding what you want to plant and will probably be influenced by your finances. But do remember that investing in shrubs will be far cheaper than moving house or having gardening help.

Of course we made the usual mistake of planting too many trees and shrubs for the size of our ground. I don't really see how this mistake can be avoided. It is human nature to want to cover the ground quickly and the rate of growth must always be a gamble. The recommended way is to interplant the expensive and long-lasting shrubs with faster growing and less expensive ones that you will weed out as necessary. Fast growing shrubs are nearly always the cheap ones.

For us these would be:

Cistus
Heather, especially daboecia
Leycesteria
Mahonia japonica
Senecio
Skimmia
Veronica (hebe)
Viburnum tinus

All these are evergreen and therefore good ground cover. The trees that have grown fastest with us are:

Eucalyptus
Prunus subhirtella 'Autumnalis'
Prunus padus
White poplar
Wild cherry, and of course birch

This latter seeds itself everywhere and need not be bought.

If you can afford brick paths amongst your shrubbery, they will be a permanent pleasure. If not, you must try to create rough paths by cutting back or mulch. They make your shrubbery more interesting. We have always thought it much more fun to plan our own garden and choose our own shrubs rather than to invoke the help of an expert. Of course, we have made many mistakes, and planted the wrong things in the wrong places. But so would they have done and charged a great deal for doing so. You can always right your mistakes by cutting down or transplanting, as long as you do the latter before they grow too large for you to handle. We find that very few shrubs object to being transplanted even in old age.

It is very sad to have to give up a vegetable garden, but the fact must be faced that vegetables make much more work than shrubs. You can grow bay laurel, sage, mint and chives with no trouble so long as you don't mind them romping away among your shrubs. I not only grow rhubarb as ground cover in the vegetable garden, I also grow it among the shrubs with gooseberries and raspberries.

We are fighting a losing battle against alpine strawberries and bluebells, but if our garden were a wood I think we should probably welcome them. I am sure that they will not hurt the larger shrubs. We have an open-work iron gate leading into our wild garden. Perhaps it should be an old wooden one overgrown with ivy. That was the gate into Frances Hodgson Burnett's "The Secret Garden" which my generation loved so much in our youth. I shall try to recapture that spirit and love the secret garden of my old age.

To Erica

How can I thank enough for all you gave?
Near sixty years of magic married love
Beyond imagining, or my deserts,
Gardening together was our dear delight.
My short dark span of loneliness is lit
By the sure knowledge that you are happy There
Eager to greet me with your lovely smile
When we are gloriously one again.

Edward